Severe Mental Illness in Autism

Brandon B. Smith

ABSTRACT

Autistic adults often experience symptoms of severe mental illness (SMI), yet research on such comorbidities remains limited. This study explored risk and protective factors for SMI among clinically and self-diagnosed autistic adults (n = 11), comparing those diagnosed in childhood with those diagnosed later in life. This study also examined their navigation of neurotypical society and perceptions of existing mental health care. Using mixed methods, the study collected quantitative survey data using the PHQ-9 and GAD-7 and qualitative interview data. Survey data was analyzed using descriptive statistics, correlation analysis, ANOVA, and ttests; interview data was analyzed through deductive and inductive thematic analysis. Statistical analyses indicated no significant correlation between age of autism spectrum disorder (ASD) diagnosis and severity of depressive or anxiety symptoms. However, autistic adults with identified support systems reported higher levels of anxiety, suggesting these systems may not fully meet their unique needs. Qualitative themes highlighted the importance of broader understanding of autism and identified protective factors against SMI as supportive communities and current linkage to mental health care. While most participants reported positive experiences with mental health care, barriers such as difficulty obtaining a clinical diagnosis, premature termination of services, and provider knowledge gaps were identified. Limitations include the small sample size and lack of a control group. Given the increasing rates of ASD diagnoses, social work clinicians must recognize the factors influencing mental health outcomes within this population. Suggestions for social work practice include increasing clinician knowledge about ASD and advocating for educational policies that impact this population. Further research should prioritize effective mental health interventions for autistic adults.

TABLE OF CONTENTS

Table of Contents

ABSTRACT 2

TABLE OF CONTENTS... 4

Chapter 1: Introduction and Conceptual FoundationsAdults with autism................ 1
Definition of Terms 1

Problem... 3

Purpose 3

Critical Race Theory and Intersectionality 4

Importance to Social Work 5

CHAPTER 2 7
The Psychological Impact of Delayed Autism Diagnosis 7
Historical Context.. 7

Hypothesized Causes of ASD 8

Social Work Perspective... 8

Existing Book on ASD 9

The Urgency of Early Diagnosis... 9

Validity of Self-Diagnosis 10

Symptomology.. 11

Autistic Experiences 13

Disparities in Autism Diagnosis 15

Prevalence of Comorbid Mental Illness Among Autistic Adults 16

ASD and Trauma 18

Mental Health Interventions for Autistic Adults 18

Disparities in Diagnosing Comorbid Mental Health Concerns 19

Risk Factors for Severe Mental Illness Among Autistic Adults 19

Pre-existing Social-Emotional Concerns 20

Substance Use 20

Protective Factors Against Severe Mental Illness Among Autistic Adults 21

Support Systems 21

Coping Skills 22

General Understanding From Wider Society 22

Experiences of and Barriers to Mental Health Care for Autistic Adults 23

METHODOLOGY 24
Procedures 25

Research Design 26

Data Analysis 26

Subject Compensation 27

RESULTS 28
Sample Demographics 28

TABLE 1. Sociodemographic Characteristics of Participants (n = 11) 30

Answering the Research Questions 31

Correlation Between Age of Diagnosis and Severity of Mental Health Concerns ..32

TABLE 3. Correlations (n = 11) 32

Age of Diagnosis and Gender 33

TABLE 4. Descriptive Statistics (n = 11) 33

TABLE 5. ANOVA 34

Relationship Between Support System and Severity of Mental Health Concerns ... 34

TABLE 6. Group Statistics (n = 11) 34

TABLE 7. Independent Samples Test 34

Protective Factors Against Severe Mental Illness Among Autistic Adults 35

Autistic Adults' Experiences With Mental Health Care 37

"It's Like Constant PMS": Struggles with Emotional Regulation 39

"We're People Just Like Everybody Else": A Need for More Understanding 43

"Social Pressure": Facilitating Socially Appropriate Behaviors 46

Coping Skills for Autistic Adults With Trauma and Mental Health Concerns 47

Prevalence of Dual Diagnoses 49

DISCUSSION 50

Summary of Key Findings 50

Limitations 53

Implications for Future Research 54

CRT and Intersectionality 54

Implications for Social Work Policy, Practice, and Advocacy 55

Conclusion 56

Chapter 1: Introduction and Conceptual FoundationsAdults with autism spectrum disorder (ASD) often find themselves dealing with cooccurring mental health challenges. While the mental health and mental health care experiences of individuals with autism have been explored in recent years, most existing research does not assess individuals with autism across the lifespan (Brown et al., 2024).

Definition of Terms

Autistic adult: Individuals over the age of 18 who have been diagnosed with autism. This Book paper uses identity-first language, as disability scholars have found that person-first language may perpetuate stigma surrounding the disorder (Gernsbacher, 2017).

Autism spectrum disorder (ASD): As defined by the *Diagnostic and Statistical Manual of Mental Disorders, Fifth Edition* (DSM-5),

A. Persistent deficits in social communication and social interaction across multiple contexts, as manifested by the following, currently or by history: deficits in socialemotional reciprocity. Deficits in nonverbal communicative behaviors are used for social interaction and in developing, maintaining, and understanding relationships.

B. Restricted, repetitive patterns of behavior, interests, or activities, as manifested by at least two of the following, currently or by history: Stereotyped or repetitive motor movements, use of objects, or speech. Insistence on sameness, inflexible adherence to routines, or ritualized patterns of verbal or nonverbal behavior. Highly restricted, fixated interests that are abnormal in intensity or focus. Hyper- or hypo reactivity to sensory input or unusual interest in sensory aspects of the environment.

C. Symptoms must be present in the early developmental period (but may not become fully manifest until social demands exceed limited capacities or may be masked by learned strategies in later life).

D. Symptoms cause clinically significant impairment in social, occupational, or other important areas of current functioning.

E. These disturbances are not better explained by intellectual disability (intellectual developmental disorder) or global developmental delay (American Psychiatric Association [APA], 2013, p. 50–51).

Camouflaging: An individual with autism's attempts to mask their autistic traits (Beck et al., 2020).

High functioning and/or *low support needs*: An individual with autism without intellectual disability and a milder symptom profile, relative to other individuals with autism (Alvares et al., 2020).

Severe mental illness (SMI): Any mental illness that seriously impacts functionality and interferes with or limits one or more major domains of life (National Institute of Mental Health [NIMH], 2024a).

Support systems: Systems or persons that offer emotional, physical, or academic support to individuals with autism (Anderson et al., 2019).

Problem

On average, autistic adults tend to report higher rates of current depression and anxiety (Arnold et al., 2019). However, current studies do not explore depression, anxiety, or other cooccurring disorders that specifically manifest as severe mental illness. Research on the mental health care experiences of autistic adults is also limited. This poses a concern as approximately 2.21% of adults, or 5,437,988 individuals, in the United States have ASD (Centers for Disease Control and Prevention [CDC], 2024b). Moreover, children are being diagnosed with ASD at an increasingly exponential rate. In 2000, approximately 1 in 150 8-year-old children were diagnosed with ASD; by 2020, however, 1 in 36 8-year-old children were diagnosed with ASD (CDC, 2024a). The implication, then, is that the rate of autistic adults will also exponentially increase in due time, as will autistic adults experiencing co-occurring mental health challenges. In 2022, 5.2% of adults in the United States had experienced serious thoughts about suicide (NIMH, 2024b). However, the autistic adult population has a fivefold increased risk for suicidal ideation; existing Book found that approximately 25.4% of adults experienced suicidal ideation within a 12-month period (Brown et al., 2024). As it stands, support for autistic adults seeking mental health treatment is lacking. The overarching themes in the existing Book about mental health care experiences among this population find that there are barriers to accessing appropriate treatment and support (Camm-Crosbie et al., 2018; Gilmore et al., 2022).

Purpose

The purpose of this project was to conduct a mixed-methods study comparing the SMI experiences of autistic adults diagnosed during childhood and autistic adults diagnosed later in life, as well as their management of SMI experiences. This study analyzed individuals with both self-diagnosed and clinically diagnosed autism. This project sought to affirm existing, though limited, Book that finds that early intervention is essential to preventing comorbid SMI later in life among autistic adults. Adults in this project's sample had low support needs (i.e., were "high functioning"). This study sought to expand the knowledge base of social workers working with the adult ASD population in mental health and integrated healthcare settings.

Critical Race Theory and Intersectionality

Critical race theory (CRT) and queer theory both emphasize the importance of unique voices (Delgado & Stefancic, 2017). However, as it stands, people of color and sexual minorities are underrepresented in who is diagnosed with ASD and who is represented in the respective research. Research shows that disparities exist in youth who are diagnosed with ASD (Yuan et al., 2021); however, research on the adult autistic population of color remains limited. There is especially a gap in the Book as it pertains to Black autistic adults (Malone et al., 2022). This is a cause for concern, as limited research means limited evidence-based practices for working with said population. Similarly, there is limited research on sexual minority autistic adults and how their sexualities impact their autistic lived experiences, which is also a cause for concern as nearly half of autistic adults (41.2%) identify as sexual minorities. On average, sexual minority autistic adults tend to have a lower quality of life than their heterosexual counterparts;

however, because research is so limited, the cause is still unknown (McQuaid et al., 2023).

The research that does exist on racialized minorities, however, suggests that Hispanic/Latine and Asian adult individuals with ASD are more likely to be misdiagnosed with psychosis (Ames et al., 2022). This could perhaps be attributed to the tenet of CRT stating that racism is ordinary (Delgado & Stefancic, 2017), that is, racial bias is ordinary throughout various domains. Therefore, White clinicians may subconsciously exhibit reduced empathy towards racialized minorities. Clinicians may contextualize clients displaying autistic traits such as restricted behaviors and blunted affect through the framework of psychosis, a highly stigmatized diagnosis, rather than assessing them holistically. It is also essential to consider the role of intersectionality when considering both racialized and sexual minority individuals with ASD.

Intersectionality refers to two or more facets of one's identities compounded to create a unique experience (Crenshaw, 1991). This is to say, the autistic lived experiences of Black individuals, for instance, are vastly different from the autistic lived experiences of White individuals based on how their racial identities interact with their diagnosis of ASD. More research must be conducted to investigate further the complexities of such compounded identities among autistic adults.

Importance to Social Work

It is imperative that social workers are knowledgeable about ASD because research shows that the primary barrier to autistic adults receiving adequate mental health care is clinicians' lack of knowledge about the disorder (Brede et al., 2022; Camm-Crosbie et al., 2018; Gilmore et al., 2022). Furthermore, with the increasing rates of children being diagnosed with ASD (CDC, 2024a), it is highly likely that social workers will, at some point in their career, receive a client with this diagnosis. Being able to provide adequate care to this population showcases a sense of competency (National Association of Social Workers [NASW], 2017).

Moreover, historically, autism has been typecast as a form of mental retardation; the disorder has only been brought to social awareness within the past 30 years thanks to films such as "Rain Man" (D'Astous et al., 2016). However, these media representations are not entirely accurate because autism exists on such a broad spectrum. Therefore, social workers must not rely solely on media depictions of autism to understand the disorder; they must educate themselves on the multitude of ways in which ASD can present. Doing so exemplifies integrity as a social worker (NASW, 2017).

While social workers have a fair understanding of interventions for clients on the spectrum, those working in welfare agencies are often not as well-informed as those in integrated healthcare settings (Karni-Visel et al., 2023). Furthermore, the autism-focused training that

social workers receive is "pretty basic" (Heslop & Bushell, 2023, p. 3227). It seems, then, that the vast amount of autism education comes from experience in the field. Social workers who are not in integrated healthcare settings but keep up to date about the existing Book on ASD to better work with the population demonstrate that they recognize the dignity and worth of all their clients (NASW, 2017).

CHAPTER 2

The Psychological Impact of Delayed Autism Diagnosis

As of 2024, approximately 5.5 million adults in the United States are diagnosed with ASD (CDC, 2024b), who tend to report higher rates of current depression and anxiety (Arnold et al., 2019). This Book review will examine the historical context of ASD, existing Book on autistic adults, risk factors for as well as protective factors against mental health concerns among autistic adults, and mental health care experiences.

Perceptions of ASD

Historical Context

Autism was first identified as an infantile disorder in 1943 by American psychiatrist Leo Kanner. Kanner described autism as an inability to form typical social contact with other individuals (Harris, 2018). Initially, being diagnosed with autism was rare; the disorder was understood as a subset of mental retardation (D'Astous et al., 2016). Bruno Bettelheim (1972), an American child psychologist, hypothesized in his book, *The Empty Fortress: Infantile Autism and the Birth of the Self*, that children develop autism due to their relationship with their mother. More specifically, Bettelheim argued that children traumatized or neglected by their mothers were at risk of developing autistic traits and could be remedied by being institutionalized indefinitely (Bettelheim, 1972). Similarly, other theorists of the era believed that autism was a reaction to toxic parental figures (Fraknoi & Ruttenberg, 1971). From the 1970s to the 1990s, profound scientific development occurred within the medical understanding of autism. The 1988 film, *Rain Man*, catapulted autism into the public view; by 1993, the disorder came to be understood as a "wide range of cognitive and neurological impairments" (D'Astous et al., 2016, p. 12). By the 2000s, autism was no longer considered a rare disorder; instead, it is estimated that approximately 1 in 54 children has the disorder (Gabis et al., 2022).

Hypothesized Causes of ASD

One major misconception is that autism is linked to vaccinations. The belief is that the mercury found in vaccinations could poison children and lead to developmental disorders. While there is evidence to support that significant amounts of neurotoxic substance during the formative years of life could cause severe developmental disorders, the amounts of mercury found in vaccinations are at negligible, non-poisonous levels; existing research correlates metal poisoning to the causation of developmental disorders (Gabis et al., 2022). Other hypothesized, and perhaps more valid, causes of ASD are environmental risk factors. Such risk factors include air pollution during pregnancy and early infancy, gestational exposure to pesticides, phthalates (Volk et al., 2022), and lithium exposure in drinking water during pregnancy (Bellinger, 2023).

Social Work Perspective

Presently, social work practice with autistic clients is focused on personalizing the experience to meet every individual's specific needs (D'Astous et al., 2016). However, according to a British exploratory study on social workers' perceptions of autism training, many do not feel adequately prepared to service the population. More autism training is needed, specifically within the social work field (Heslop & Bushell, 2023; Karni-Visel et al., 2023).

Existing Book on ASD

This section will explore the existing Book on diagnosis timing, self-diagnosis, symptomology, autistic experiences, disparities in autism diagnosis, prevalence of comorbidities, autism and trauma, mental health interventions, risk factors for mental health concerns, protective factors against mental health concerns, and experiences of and barriers to accessing mental health care among autistic adults.

The Urgency of Early Diagnosis

Whereas an early diagnosis accounts for social differences among autistic children, later autism diagnosis is linked to poorer mental health and feeling othered. In a qualitative study of 10 adult men in South Africa who were diagnosed with ASD at age 18 or older, all participants expressed that the lack of early diagnosis significantly impacted their lives. The men expressed experiencing emotional and physical bullying by classmates, academic difficulty due to issues with concentration and motor skills, and feeling misunderstood by their peers and adults in their lives (Lupindo et al., 2023). Meanwhile, an adult autistic woman in a British study expressed that her undiagnosed autism placed her in precarious situations, saying, "Had I known about Asperger's, I think I'd have known that I'm more suggestible…and I might not have ended up in the situations that I did" (Bargiela et al., 2016, p. 3286). In fact, 9 of the 14 women in this study reported experiences of sexual abuse, citing social mimicry, difficulty reading social cues and assessing safety risks, and desperation for social acceptance as the risks that placed them in these situations.

In both samples, autistic adults reported high rates of depression; in the male sample, there were also high rates of suicidal ideation (Bargiela et al., 2016; Lupindo et al., 2022).

Moreover, in a longitudinal study where baseline data were collected from 295 autistic adults in Australia, the majority (90%) were diagnosed in adulthood. Of this sample, 52% scored above the depression cut-off on the PHQ-9 (Arnold et al., 2019). In another study of 77 adults diagnosed with autism later in life, the themes that emerged included feeling different and struggling to maintain a sense of normalcy, especially within their romantic and platonic relationships. Self-reported depression was also prevalent among this participant sample (Lewis, 2016b).

Validity of Self-Diagnosis

Because many individuals on the autism spectrum do not receive early diagnosis, many undiagnosed adults resort to self-diagnosis. In a study of 37 adult individuals who were not formally diagnosed, self-diagnosis was crucial to facilitate participants' understanding of themselves; without this understanding, participants reported feeling othered and isolated (Lewis, 2016a). Some theorists argue that individuals who may feel othered throughout their lives resort to self-diagnosis because of identifying with autism portrayals in mainstream media (Mittman et al., 2023).

Symptomology

Currently, the symptomology of ASD is defined as deficits in social communication and interactions across multiple domains of life and at least two repetitive and restricted patterns of behavior (APA, 2013, pp. 50–51).

Deficits in social communication. Social communication difficulties are a core component of ASD. According to the DSM-5, individuals who are diagnosed with ASD must present with difficulties in social emotional reciprocity (e.g., trouble with social approach and maintaining conversations); nonverbal communication (e.g., abnormal eye contact and difficulty understanding body language); and developing and maintaining interpersonal relationships (APA, 2013). These social communication deficits lead to significant differences in empathy, with autistic individuals possessing lower rates of empathy and difficulties with facial emotion recognition (Spain & Blainey, 2015). Social communication deficits also complicate employment opportunities for autistic adults; only 20% to 55% of autistic adults in various studies reviewed by a team of researchers were employed (Gray et al., 2014). Social communication deficits are also linked to marked executive dysfunction, which can also hinder independent living and finding employment. In fact, research shows that executive dysfunction can explain 20%-60% of the variance in social functioning and community (Baker-Ericzén et al., 2018).

Restricted and repetitive patterns of behavior and interests. Restricted and repetitive patterns of behaviors and interests are another facet of ASD. According to the DSM-5, individuals must present with a minimum of 2 out of the following 4 behaviors to be diagnosed with ASD: repetitive motor movements and speech; rigid adherence to routines; highly specific interests with abnormal focus; and increased or decreased reactions to sensory input (APA, 2013). One study of 15 autistic adults found that indulging in these restricted and repetitive behaviors and interests is a useful method for autistic adults to manage anxiety. Moreover, repetitive and restricted behaviors and interests are seen as integral to their identities (Long et al., 2024) and in another study of 687 adults with autism, 443 participants, or 65% of the total sample, reported having a special interest (i.e., restricted interests); 82% of these participants reported having more than one special interest. Common special interests among the sample included computers, gaming, and music. Women were significantly more likely to have introspective special interests, such as autism and psychology, whereas men were more likely to be interested in a wide range of activities. Across the sample, most participants did not perceive their special interests as an obstacle to daily functioning, but instead felt positively impacted by them. In fact, participants who were motivated to engage in their special interests reported increased subjective well-being (Grove et al., 2018).

Emotional dysregulation. ASD often occurs with high rates of comorbid internalizing and externalizing behaviors, such as impaired emotional regulation which results in difficulty modulating emotional responses (Richey et al., 2015). Autistic individuals also tend to struggle with alexithymia, or difficulty in identifying and describing their emotions. Autistic individuals who struggle with alexithymia tend to focus on external, rather than internal, experiences when attempting to describe their emotions. In a study of 64 young adults with ASD, researchers found that participants who experienced alexithymia also experienced worsened emotional regulation, which then contributed to elevated rates of anxiety and depressive symptoms (Morie et al., 2019).

Autistic Experiences

Being that ASD is marked by social differences, autistic adults by and large report schooling and workplace experiences unique to that of non-autistic adults.

School experiences. A study of 28 autistic secondary school students–14 autistic, 14 (age and gender matched) non-autistic–analyzed their respective schooling experiences and found no significant differences between the autistic sample's and the control group's perceptions of school staff. However, 12 of the 14 autistic participants reported that their peers are their biggest distractors in class, with one participant stating, "friends mess about and distract me" (Dillon et al., 2016, p. 226); the control group did not focus as much on peer relations. Both samples spoke highly of group activities within the classroom setting, but autistic participants were more likely to report only having one or a few close friends, compared to control participants who reported larger peer groups (Dillon et al., 2016). In an analysis of various studies which reviewed youth well-being as it related to their school experiences, students also generally reported positive experiences with school staff. However, support from special education teachers and support

staff such as paraprofessionals may foster negative emotions among autistic students if poorly managed and students feel singled out, Moreover, like Dillon et al.'s (2016) findings regarding autistic students being distracted by their peers, students with ASD experienced negative emotions due to the sensory input of the school environment. Students with ASD, according to this Book review, also found themselves victims of bullying by their peers (Danker et al., 2016). By contrast, college is a more positive experience for adults with autism. In fact, many adults report thriving due to supports such as academic advisors, counseling centers, tutors, officers of disability services, and professors (Anderson et al., 2019).

Employment experiences. A 2021 study found that 24% of autistic youth (14-21 years of age) had a paid work experience within the past year at the time of the study. This study found that autistic youth who had a household income of $120,000 were nearly 3 times more likely to experience employment during their adolescent years compared to youth from families with household incomes less than $40,000 a year, hinting that familial connections assist autistic youth in securing employment (Qian et al., 2021). In another study, a major theme that emerged among autistic adults on an online forum is the experience of workplace anxiety. Like the schooling experiences of autistic individuals, a common thread among employed autistic adults is overstimulation within the workplace, whether it be through work overload, long working hours, lack of stable routine, or excessive sensory input from the physical environment. When factoring for gendered differences, researchers found that whereas women were more concerned with social interaction and interpersonal communication, men struggled more with executive dysfunction and disclosing their autism diagnosis (Nagib & Wilton, 2021). When autistic adults do choose to disclose their diagnosis within the workplace, most opt to disclose their diagnosis selectively. However, only about a third reported that disclosure had positive outcomes; all other participants reported that their disclosure experience was neutral or negative. Those who did report a negative disclosure experience expressed facing bullying and purposeful discrimination as a direct result of sharing their diagnosis (Romualdez et al., 2021).

Disparities in Autism Diagnosis

Disparities in who is diagnosed with ASD and their subsequent experiences have been documented across existing Book. Research suggests that White males are much more likely to receive an ASD diagnosis (Durkin et al., 2017; Yuan et al., 2021), while girls and adults seeking diagnosis are often dismissed due to high rates of camouflaging (Beck et al., 2020;

Lehnhardt et al., 2016).

Gender. In a United States sample of autistic children aged 3 to 17, males were 4 times more likely to be diagnosed with autism (Yuan et al., 2021). This could be because autism presents differently in males and females. In a study of 107 autistic adults diagnosed during adulthood, females showed significantly fewer processing speech impairments than their male counterparts. Additionally, females reported twice as many intimate partnerships as males in this study (Lehnhardt et al., 2016). These statistics can be attributed to autistic women's tendency to camouflage their autism to conform to social expectations (e.g., avoiding topics of special interest in conversation to make and maintain friendships; Beck et al., 2020). However, these efforts to camouflage may hinder a formal diagnosis: in an English study of 109 survey respondents with autism ages 16-25 years old, adults with autism felt that being perceived as “too ‘normal” (i.e., camouflaging well) delays diagnosis (Crane et al., 2019, p. 484).

Race. Historically, White individuals are more likely to receive an autism diagnosis; Durkin et al.’s (2017) study analyzing data from 2002-2010 found that White children were 19% more likely to receive an autism diagnosis than their Black counterparts and 65% more likely to receive a diagnosis than Hispanic/Latine children. According to a cross-sectional U.S. study using nationally representative data from 2014 to 2019, however, the disparity between nonHispanic/Latine White individuals ages 3-17 and Black individuals ages 3-17 diagnosed with ASD has grown smaller due to an increase in Black children diagnosed in 2018. Of the three racialized groups, Hispanic/Latine children were the least likely to be diagnosed with ASD

(Yuan et al., 2021).

Prevalence of Comorbid Mental Illness Among Autistic Adults

Autistic adults were more likely to be diagnosed with more psychiatric conditions than non-autistic adults of the same ethnicity (Ames et al., 2022). Crane et al. (2019) found that

80.7% of survey respondents with autism had previously experienced mental health problems.

Depression and suicidality. Autistic adults are at an increased risk for depression and suicidal behavior. In a longitudinal study of Australian adults with autism, autistic adults scored significantly higher on measures of current depression and anxiety than controls (Arnold et al., 2019). Furthermore, according to a systematic review of Book from 2018 to 2024 on suicidality among autistic adults, autistic adults have up to an eightfold increased risk of death by suicide when compared to non-autistic adults (Brown et al., 2024). In line with these findings, in a study of 63 autistic new patients in a psychiatric outpatient setting, nearly a third of patients (31%) in a study reported suicidal ideation within the past month; nearly 9 in 10 (86%) reported lifetime suicidal ideation; and 1 in 4 (25%) reported at least one suicide attempt. Moreover, nearly half (44%) reported non-suicidal self-injury (Nyrenius et al., 2023). Suicidality is especially increased among women who engage in camouflaging behaviors to a high degree (Beck et al., 2020); that is, autistic individuals who repress their autistic traits are more likely to experience suicidal ideation and behaviors

Other mental illness. Autistic adults are also at an increased risk for mental illness aside from depression. In a longitudinal study of 68 autistic adults aged 19-80, 71% experienced at least one other co-occurring condition, and 37% met the criteria for three or more co-occurring conditions. Furthermore, this study found that mental health concerns persisted into older age and did not improve over time, generally speaking (Roestorf et al., 2022). Similarly, in Bargiela et al.'s (2016) study, nearly all participants expressed experiencing mental health difficulties such as anxiety and eating disorders. More specifically, in a systemic review of the Book published between 2017 and 2022, researchers found that the most reported comorbid mental health issues besides depression were ADHD, with 25%-38% of the sample surveyed having a dual diagnosis of anxiety (20%) and OCD (5%; Gilmore et al., 2022).

ASD and Trauma

Research shows that individuals with ASD have an increased risk of exposure to trauma, especially regarding physical and sexual abuse (Bargiela et al., 2016; Rumball et al., 2021). Autistic adults also have higher rates of trauma exposure, with 63% of an autistic research sample reporting four or more traumas compared to only 34% of the non-autistic control group. Furthermore, autistic adults are significantly more likely to develop post-traumatic stress disorder (PTSD) symptoms after exposure to a traumatic event compared to non-autistic adults (Hume & Burgess, 2021). In fact, whereas only 5% of the control group reported probable PTSD, 45% of the autistic sample reported probable PTSD following a traumatic event (Rumball et al., 2021). Another study by Kerns et al. (2022) found that, while traditionally assessed sources of trauma (e.g., physical abuse, housing instability) were cited as sources of childhood trauma, social exclusion was a central theme among autistic adults with childhood trauma. This social exclusion manifested as bullying, social isolation, and alienation among peers. Another central theme that arose was being physically or psychologically trapped (i.e., being physically restrained or feeling a loss of autonomy in therapeutic environments; Kerns et al., 2022).

Mental Health Interventions for Autistic Adults

Existing research shows that existing mental health interventions used with non-autistic adults suffice for autistic adults, as well. However, research also finds that for mental health interventions to be most effective, they should be modified to meet the specific needs of autistic adults. A systematic review of 13 English-language studies analyzing autistic adults found that mental health interventions are most successful for autistic adults when they are facilitated by clinicians who acknowledge that mental health outcomes and responses to interventions will appear different for adults on the autism spectrum. As such, interventions should be adapted to fit the specific needs of the adult with ASD, as ASD has a variety of manifestations. Mental health interventions are also most effective when delivered by clinicians with prior experience working with patients with ASD (Moore et al., 2024). Similarly, Han et al. (2023) found that autistic adults report group interventions as a barrier to mental health care due to social communication difficulties.

Disparities in Diagnosing Comorbid Mental Health Concerns

Race and sexuality as they relate to autism in adults often lead to disparities in the acknowledgement of comorbid mental health concerns. For instance, a 2022 study that analyzed patients of Kaiser Permanente Northern California members enrolled between 2008 and 2012 with a diagnosis of ASD found that Black, Hispanic/Latine, and Asian adults were less likely to be diagnosed with psychiatric conditions compared to their White counterparts (Ames et al., 2022). Furthermore, in a survey completed by 651 autistic adults, participants who identified as a sexual minority reported poorer mental health and quality of life when compared to heterosexual autistic adults. This is especially concerning because 41.2% of the sample surveyed identified as a sexual minority (McQuaid et al., 2023).

Risk Factors for Severe Mental Illness Among Autistic Adults

Current Book suggests that risk factors for severe mental illness, for instance, suicidality, among autistic adults include comorbid diagnoses, poor self-perception, camouflaging, denial, and illicit substance use (Beck et al., 2020; Brown et al., 2024; Nyrenius et al., 2023).

Pre-existing Social-Emotional Concerns

Social-emotional concerns such as pre-existing comorbid diagnoses, poor self-perception, and camouflaging increase the risk of other mental health concerns among autistic adults. According to Brown et al. (2024), autistic adults with comorbid psychiatric disorders such as borderline personality disorder, bipolar disorder, psychosis, and adjustment disorder showed positive associations with elevated risk of suicidal thoughts and behaviors. Perceived loneliness, bullying, and interpersonal conflicts were also reported to increase risk for suicidal thoughts and behaviors (Brown et al., 2024). Other risk factors for suicidal thoughts and behaviors include low self-esteem, alexithymia, emotional dysregulation, internalizing and externalizing problems, nonsuicidal self-injurious behavior, lower levels of cognitive control, and camouflaging (Andersen et al., 2023; Brown et al., 2024). Similarly, Beck et al. (2020) found in a sample of 59 women with self-reported autistic traits that camouflaging was significantly associated with psychological distress, even when accounting for the number of autistic traits. Furthermore, a longitudinal study analyzing the coping strategies of autistic adults aged 16 to 80 found that adults who engaged in denial and self-blaming behaviors had higher rates of anxiety and depression (Muniandy et al., 2023).

Substance Use

Autistic adults are at higher risk of abusing illicit substances: Huang et al.'s (2021) longitudinal study following Taiwanese adults with autism over 16 years found that autistic adults had a higher risk of substance use disorder when compared to non-autistic controls, including those with the same comorbidities. Similarly, in a study of 63 psychiatric outpatient autistic adults, 19 participants presented with harmful or hazardous alcohol/drug use. Of these 19, only 2 out of 13 women and 4 out of 6 men had a clinical diagnosis of substance abuse. Still, high self-reported consumption of drugs and/or alcohol explained up to a third in the variance of suicide attempts (Nyrenius et al., 2023).

Protective Factors Against Severe Mental Illness Among Autistic Adults

Protective factors against severe mental illness include identified support systems, therapeutic coping skills, exercise, and feeling understood by others (Bernate et al., 2024; Han et al., 2023; Huang et al., 2021; Muniandy et al., 2023).

Support Systems

Autistic adults with a strong self-identified support system are more likely to have an improved quality of life and, thus, fewer mental health concerns. An online qualitative methods study collected data from over a thousand online forum discussion posts from college students with ASD from 2012 and 2013 and found that college students with ASD identified their academic advisors, counseling centers, tutors, disability services, and professors as main support systems while navigating college life (Anderson et al., 2019). Outside of college settings, autistic adults value their friendships with other autistic adults, and they feel more understood by them. As one participant in a qualitative study analyzing adults' support after autism diagnosis put it,

"It is important to get validation from shared idiosyncrasies and experiences, but also vital for personal growth to have opportunities to discover unique differences, be it within one's own tribe or not" (Huang et al., 2021, p. 1164). Participants with intellectual disability, in comparison, benefitted less from friendships with other autistic adults and more from relationships with family members (Huang et al., 2021).

Coping Skills

Autistic adults with reliable skills to cope with life's stressors are also less likely to develop comorbid mental health concerns. Problem-solving and acceptance skills predicted higher rates of well-being among autistic adults. Moreover, sustained engagement in positive coping skills such as problem-solving and acceptance predicted better mental well-being 2 years after initiating coping skills (Muniandy et al., 2023). Furthermore, a study of four autistic adults ages 22 to 39 found that physical exercise assisted in emotional regulation via motor concentration and self-control (Bernate et al., 2024).

General Understanding From Wider Society

A British mixed-methods study interviewed 144 adults with ASD about how to mitigate stigma related to their diagnosis and found overarching themes including "autism is not widely understood" and "the main solution for stigma is education of wider society" (Han et al., 2023, p. 1682). Furthermore, many participants in an English study of twenty-one young autistic people reported difficulties navigating a neurotypical (i.e., non-autistic) world. Pressure to act "normal," according to participants, led to comorbid mental health conditions (Crane et al., 2019). The implication, then, is that a society with a better understanding of ASD would prevent comorbidities.

Experiences of and Barriers to Mental Health Care for Autistic Adults

In Crane et al.'s (2019) study, 90.1% of survey respondents with autism reported previously seeking mental health care; however, their experiences vary. A systematic review of 38 studies analyzing adults with ASD's experiences with mental health care found that, for participants, accessing care is too complex. Practitioners also observed mental health services being reluctant to work with autistic adults (Brede et al., 2022). Similarly, a systematic review of Book dated 2017-2022 on adults with autism's use of mental health care found that providers lack knowledge on ASD, treatment is not suited to accommodate individual needs, and there is difficulty navigating the health care system. Additionally, there could be physical barriers to attending a mental health care clinic, depending on the autistic individual's needs (e.g., "not wanting to sit in the waiting area due to sensory overload"; Gilmore et al., 2022, p. 18). Moreover, a study of 200 autistic adults ages 18-67 without intellectual disability found that participants had trouble accessing treatment and support, felt that practitioners lacked understanding of autistic people with comorbidities, and felt that there was a lack of appropriate treatment and support (Camm-Crosbie et al., 2018). The research outlined in this Book establishes the foundation for the study described in Chapters 3 and 4.

CHAPTER 3

METHODOLOGY

This study addressed the following questions:

1. Is there an association between age at time of ASD diagnosis and severity of presenting mental health concerns?
2. What, if any, association is there between age at time of ASD diagnosis and gender?
3. Is there a relationship between identified support systems and the severity of presenting mental health concerns?
4. What protective factors exist for severe mental illness among adults diagnosed with ASD?
5. How do autistic adults perceive existing mental health care?

This section reviews participant requirements, recruitment, procedures for obtaining consent, and data analysis.

Participants

The participants in this study consisted of 11 individuals who met the following criteria: (a) are 18 years of age or older, (b) are clinically or self-diagnosed with ASD, (c) currently reside in the United States, (d) do not exhibit symptoms of psychosis and can speak and understand English. The exclusion criteria for this study were as follows: (a) do not meet criteria for ASD and (b) currently exhibiting symptoms of psychosis.

Recruitment

After receiving Institutional Review Board approval, personal social networks were utilized to recruit participants. A recruitment flyer was posted on the researcher's personal social media page to locate a key informant. The Bob Murphy Access Center, the student disability services office on the California State University, Long Beach campus, was also utilized as a key informant. Interested participants contacted the researcher via email address. Phone calls were then coordinated with interested potential participants using Google Voice to screen for eligibility. Data was not collected during the screening process. If any participants were not eligible, any screening data were destroyed. After the screening process, eligible and willing participants scheduled a date and time to interview and choose the modality of their interview (Zoom or telephone).

Procedures

Informed consent was obtained via Zoom or telephone, depending on the participant's chosen method of interview. Informed consent was read to participants prior to the interview and/or participants received informed consent via chat without requiring a signature; it was also on Qualtrics. Any participant questions were answered upon hearing the informed consent form.

Participants then provided verbal consent.

Participants who opted for a Zoom interview were asked to turn off their cameras and use a pseudonym on the application to ensure confidentiality. Participants who opted for a telephone interview were asked to dial my Google Voice number, prefacing it with *67 to hide the caller ID to ensure confidentiality. Data was transcribed and saved under a pseudonym. Data was stored securely on a USB drive in a locked drawer.

Research Design

The research design was mixed methods, utilizing both a qualitative interview and quantitative survey questionnaire. The survey questionnaire was distributed to participants via text message prior to the qualitative interview. The survey questionnaire asked participants demographic questions including (a) gender, (b) race/ethnicity, (c) sexual orientation, (d) primary source of income, (e) relationship status, and (f) housing arrangement. It also assessed participants' rates of depression, anxiety over the past 2 weeks using the PHQ-9 and the GAD-7. For this study, a score of 15 or higher on the PHQ-9 is considered severe depression; a score of

15 or higher on the GAD-7 is considered severe anxiety (Kroenke et al., 1999; Spitzer et al., 2006). The Qualtrics form was set up so that responses were anonymous. Participants were free to go back at any time during the survey.

Interviews lasted 30-90 minutes and were conducted via Zoom or telephone. Participants were asked a series of questions regarding their diagnosis of ASD, their experiences with ASD, their experiences in social settings, their mental health care experiences, any major life stressors, and their support systems.

Data Analysis

Data from the survey questionnaires was input into SPSS 28 to produce descriptive statistics of the demographic information collected, calculate Pearson's correlation coefficient to test for research question #1, one-way analysis of variance to test for research question #2, and independent t-tests for research question #3. Data from the interviews was coded deductively to determine protective factors and perceptions of mental health care among autistic adults, per research questions #4 and #5. Data from the interviews was also coded inductively to identify any other significant emerging themes.

Subject Compensation

Subjects were compensated for their time with a $15 gift card to a retailer of their choice if they responded to all demographic questions during the survey and at least 11 out of 13

questions during the interview.

CHAPTER 4

RESULTS

This chapter will discuss the sample's demographics, interpret statistics on collected survey data to explore research questions one to three, and review overarching themes found in the interview data related to research questions four and five.

Sample Demographics

The ages of participants are presented in Table 1. The 11 study participants ranged in age from 19 to 37, with an average age of 27 (*SD* = 6.57). Data is missing from one participant. The demographic characteristics of the participants are presented in Table 2. Participants consisted of seven (64%) cisgender females, two (18%) cisgender males, and two (18%) individuals identifying as nonbinary or gender non-conforming. No transgender females or transgender males participated in the study. The largest racial or ethnic group in the sample was Hispanic/Latine (55%), followed by White (27%) and Asian (18%). No Black African American, Native Hawaiian, or Pacific Islander individuals participated in the study. Over half of the sample identified as bisexual/pansexual (55%), followed by heterosexual (36%) and asexual (9%). No gay or lesbian individuals or individuals identifying with another sexual orientation participated in this study. Eight individuals were employed (80%) at the time of participation; one individual was receiving social security income (10%), and another was receiving financial support from their family (10%). Data is missing from one participant. Five participants reported being single (46%) at the time of participation, four participants reported being in a romantic relationship (36%), and two participants reported being married (18%). No participants reported being divorced or widowed. Four participants reported living with friends or family (36%) at the time of participation, three reported being homeowners (27%), two reported renting (18%), and two reported other living arrangements (18%). No participants reported being unhoused.

TABLE 1. Sociodemographic Characteristics of Participants ($n = 11$)

Demographics	f	%
Gender		
Cisgender female (assigned female at birth, identifies as female)	7	64%
Cisgender male (assigned male at birth, identifies as male)	2	18%
Nonbinary/gender non-conforming (does not identify as male or female)	2	18%
Race/Ethnicity		
White	3	27%
Hispanic or Latine	6	55%
Asian	2	18%
Sexual orientation		
Heterosexual	4	36%
Bisexual/Pansexual	6	55%
Asexual	1	9%
Primary source of income		
Work	8	80%
SSI	1	10%
Familial support	1	10%
Missing/Unknown	1	10%
Relationship status		
Single	5	46%
In a relationship	4	36%
Married	2	18%
Housing arrangement		
Rent	2	18%
Own	3	27%

Stay with friends/family	4	36%
Other	2	18%

Information regarding diagnosis is listed in Table 2. Participants reported being diagnosed with ASD from ages 4 to 46, with a mean of 22.36 years old (*SD*=12.52). Seven

(64%) participants were clinically diagnosed, and four (36%) were self-diagnosed.

TABLE 2. Information on Diagnosis (*n* = 11)

Demographics	*f*	%	Mean	*SD*
Age of Diagnosis			22.36	12.52
Clinically Diagnosed	7	64%		
Self-Diagnosed	4	36%		

Answering the Research Questions

This research sought to answer five primary questions using a mixed-methods approach. Among these questions were: is there an association between age at the time of ASD diagnosis and severity of presenting mental health concerns? Is there an association between age at time of ASD diagnosis and gender? Is there a relationship between identified support systems and the severity of mental health concerns? This section addressed these three research questions using quantitative data analysis. The remaining research questions were addressed by using deductive thematic analysis: what are the protective factors against severe mental illness among adults diagnosed with ASD? And how do autistic adults perceive existing mental health care?

Correlation Between Age of Diagnosis and Severity of Mental Health Concerns

Data from the PHQ-9 and GAD-7 were totaled to measure the severity of mental health concerns. PHQ-9 scores of 15 or above and GAD-7 scores of 10 or above were cause for concern. Pearson's correlation coefficient was then used to determine if there was a correlation between these scores and the age of diagnosis (see Table 3).

TABLE 3. Correlations (*n* = 11)

		Age of Diagnosis	PHQ-9 score	GAD-7 score
Age of Diagnosis	Pearson Correlation	1	-.255	.187
	Sig. (2-tailed)		.449	.582
	n	11	11	11
PHQ-9 score	Pearson Correlation	-.255	1	.537
	Sig. (2-tailed)	.449		.089
	n	11	11	11
GAD-7 score	Pearson Correlation	.187	.537	1
	Sig. (2-tailed)	.582	.089	
	n	11	11	11

Results indicated no significant correlation between age of diagnosis and PHQ-9 scores (*r*

(11) = -0.255, p = .449) or GAD-7 scores (r (11) = 0.187, p = .582). There was also no statistically significant correlation between PHQ-9 and GAD-7 scores (r (11) = 0.537, p = .089), though the data neared significance, suggesting a potential relationship between depressive and anxiety symptoms.

Age of Diagnosis and Gender

A one-way ANOVA was conducted to examine differences in age of diagnosis across the gender spectrum (Tables 4 and 5). The results indicated no statistically significant differences in age of diagnosis across genders, F (2, 8) = 2.27, p = .166. However, descriptive statistics showed that cisgender females (M = 27.71, SD = 12.13) had a higher mean age of diagnosis than cisgender males (M = 11.00, SD = 9.90) and nonbinary/gender non-conforming individuals (M = 15.00, SD = 4.24), suggesting that cisgender females are often diagnosed with ASD later in life.

TABLE 4. Descriptive Statistics (n = 11)

Age of Diagnosis	*M*	*SD*
Cisgender female (assigned female at birth, identifies as female)	27.71	12.13
Cisgender male (assigned male at birth, identifies as male)	11.0	9.89
Nonbinary/gender non-conforming (does not identify as male or female)	15.0	4.24
Total	22.36	12.51

TABLE 5. ANOVA

	Sum of Squares	*df*	Mean Square	*F*	*p*
Between Groups	567.117	2	283.558	2.27	.166
Within Groups	999.429	8	124.929		
Total	1566.545	10			

Relationship Between Support System and Severity of Mental Health Concerns

A series of independent sample *t*-tests were conducted to examine the differences in the severity of mental health concerns among autistic adults who identified current support systems and those who did not (Tables 6 and 7).

TABLE 6. Group Statistics (n = 11)

	Support system	*n*	Mean	Std. Deviation	Std. Error Mean
PHQ-9 score	Yes	7	12.14	5.11301	1.93
	No	4	10.00	5.77	2.88
GAD-7 score	Yes	7	12.14	4.61	1.72
	No	4	6.00	3.16	1.58

TABLE 7. Independent Samples Test

	Support System	
		95% Confidence Interval of the Difference
Sig.		

		(2tailed)	Mean Difference	Std. Error Difference	Lower	Upper
PHQ-9 score	Equal variances assumed	.538	2.14	3.34	-5.43183	9.71754
GAD-7 score	Equal variances assumed	.042*	6.14	2.59	.26141	12.02431

**Significant at p < .05 level.*

For PHQ-9 scores, participants with support systems (*M* = 12.14, *SD* = 5.11) did not differ significantly from those without support systems (*M* = 10.00, *SD* = 5.77), *t* (9) = 0.64, *p* = .538, 95% *CI* [-5.43, 9.72]. Levene's test indicated equal variances (*F* = 0.085, *p* = .777). For GAD-7 scores, there was a significant difference between groups. Participants with support systems (*M* = 12.14, *SD* = 4.56) reported significantly higher anxiety levels than those without support systems (*M* = 6.00, *SD* = 3.16), *t* (9) = 2.36, *p* = .042, 95% *CI* [0.26, 12.02]. Levene's test indicated equal variances (*F* = 0.784, *p* = .399). These findings suggest that there is no significant difference between the rates of depressive symptoms and the perceived strength of support systems among autistic adults. However, it is suggested that autistic adults with identified support systems average higher rates of anxiety symptoms.

Protective Factors Against Severe Mental Illness Among Autistic Adults

The protective factors against severe mental illness which were identified among the current sample include having a history of supportive communities, receiving mental health care at the time of the study, and personal resilience.

History of supportive community. Three of the 11 (27%) participants did not report any history of severe mental illness. Two of these 3 reported a history of supportive communities outside of family and mental health care teams. John, a 20-year-old male participant clinically diagnosed with ASD at age 4, reported being a part of the Boys and Girls Club in elementary and middle school and joining an autism-focused program at his community college. John reported building friendships as a child through the Boys and Girls Club. He also spoke positively about the autism-focused program at his community college:

> I did an autism program [at community college]…we meet every Friday, 10 to 11:30, to just talk about different autistic topics, and events as well…we did one on, like, relationships, like, friends…and like, how to do it properly…and then some fun events, like a Mario Kart tournament.

Jennifer, a female participant clinically diagnosed with ASD at age 46 (current age unknown), reported having a sponsor in Al-Anon due to her ex-husband's struggle with alcoholism. She viewed her relationship with her sponsor as beneficial: "I went to Al-Anon… just so eye-opening. And I have an Al-Anon sponsor there, and then I have a small set of close friends, and we all support each other." Other identified supports across the sample included family, romantic partners, friends, and therapy.

Current mental health care. Four of the 11 (36%) participants reported seeing a therapist at the time of participations. Two of these 4 participants reported no history of severe mental illness, one reported a history of active suicidal ideation, and one reported a history of suicide attempts. Both participants without a history of severe mental illness reported weekly sessions with a therapist. The remaining two participants reported positive relationships with their therapists. Fatima, a 34-year-old woman clinically diagnosed with ASD at age 33, shared that she had been seeing the same therapist for 4 years, who ultimately referred her for an autism assessment. Derek, a 21-year-old male self-diagnosed with ASD at 18, also reported positive mental health care experiences since his most recent suicide attempt:

> Being in therapy is the biggest [support], and it has been extremely helpful. So. I was just I used to struggle with therapy a lot because I would never really click with my therapist or the groups I would [do would] just not work for me. The place that I'm at now, my therapist, is amazing.

Personal resilience. Two of the 3 (67%) participants who did not report a history of severe mental illness expressed personal resilience. Chase, a 37-year-old nonbinary individual clinically diagnosed with ASD at age 12, shared: "I've had thoughts there's, like, depressive thoughts, suicidal thoughts throughout, like, over the years. Sometimes that comes up, but then they often, like, disappear." Meanwhile, Jennifer shared:

> I don't understand suicide. I don't get it. I don't because today can be the worst day of your life, right? Today can, like, kick rocks. It could be horrible and tomorrow could be the best day of your life, but if you give up, if you commit suicide, you don't get a chance to experience that.

Autistic Adults' Experiences With Mental Health Care

Contrary to existing Book, most of the autistic adults (9 out of 11; 82% of participants) in this sample reported positive mental health care experiences. One participant reported solely negative mental health care experiences, stating, "Honestly, I think I might have had people that shouldn't have been therapists" (Andrea, 19-year-old nonbinary individual (she/her) clinically diagnosed with ASD at age 18). She recounted a specific instance following two suicide attempts at age

16 where a therapist told her, "'that's kind of, like, the reality of…life, like, some people…have, like, you know, one attempt, and then they…sort of move on from it." Another participant–Paula, a 26-year-old woman (she/they) self-diagnosed with ASD at age 24–reported never having utilized therapeutic services. Various barriers to accessing mental health care were identified by participants, among those being accessing ASD diagnosis, premature termination of therapeutic services, and internalized stigma.

Barriers to autism diagnosis. Three of the 11 (27%) participants reported difficulties in obtaining a clinical ASD diagnosis. As succinctly put by Jessie, a 35-year-old woman diagnosed by her therapist, the overarching theme is "it should be made easier to get diagnosed." Paula, who is self-diagnosed, shared that she opted for self-diagnosis due to the financial cost of obtaining a clinical diagnosis: "Maybe I should get tested, but finding out that testing is actually kind of expensive, even with insurance. So just, you know, [I did] all the online testing that I can do for free." Meanwhile, Jennifer cited gender differences as a barrier to being diagnosed with ASD earlier in her life:

> ASD was diagnosed a lot in the 80s and 90s, when I was young, you know, for boys, so for us girls, if we displayed anything like that, we were told that we're being difficult, we're too sensitive, we're this, we're that.

Premature termination of services. Three of the 11 (27%) participants reported premature termination of therapeutic services for several reasons. Chelsea, a 26-year-old woman self-diagnosed with ASD at age 24, cited financial circumstances as the reason why she prematurely discontinued her therapeutic services: "Honestly, insurance is a severe hit or miss… I'd do [therapy] for a time;

then I think I lost insurance or couldn't afford it at the time." Meanwhile, both Chase and Jessie reported building positive working relationships with their respective therapists before their services were terminated due to the clinician retiring.

Lack of knowledge about autism from mental health care practitioners. One participant, Andrea, expressed dissatisfaction with her experiences with mental health care due to practitioners' lack of knowledge regarding ASD. When speaking of her experiences calling a crisis hotline, she said:

> [The crisis hotlines] were kind of helpful, but kind of not because I didn't really I felt like the ways that I was, like, struggling, like a lot of people didn't understand, because it was like, obviously, like, the autistic experience is not something that a lot of people would understand, considering that statistically low people like, have it, few people have it.

Internalized stigma. One participant, Paula, reported not receiving mental health services due to internalized feelings of shame: "I feel embarrassed that I'm gonna dump on this person, even though this is her job, embarrassed to let them in." They also expressed the feeling that they must "[wait] for something, like, really bad to happen, where I really desperately need, like, a session."

Inductive Thematic Analysis

"It's Like Constant PMS": Struggles with Emotional Regulation

Nine of the 11 (82%) participants reported struggling with emotional regulation at some point in their lives. Six of these 9 (67%) participants reported struggling with explosive anger. Participants attributed their bouts of anger to disturbances in their repetitive and restricted behaviors and being easily irritable. As

Fatima elaborated, "I get very angry and frustrated, like a level…between frustrated and legitimately really angry when I don't do things in a certain way." These bouts of anger present uniquely among the participants; however, the overarching theme is that emotions are felt at an extreme intensity. For instance, Chelsea shared:

> Sometimes, I would just wind myself up so much…I either yell or get really attitude-y, and then full breakdown, tears, sitting on the floor, feel like a complete fool, because I don't know what's happening with my life. It's like constant PMS.

In a similar vein, Derek shared that, prior to beginning therapeutic services, "it was definitely hard to keep everything at bay." Over a third (36%) of participants were also more inclined to express anger in the home towards familiar individuals. Marcia shared that, as a child, she would "fight with [her] sister all the time, [her] brother, [her] parents"; Chelsea shared that she tends to "full on snap" at "the people [she lives] with." John explained that he tends to express anger towards his parents because "at home, [he is] more, like, comfortable, like, yelling."

"It Gave Me Purpose": Advantages and Disadvantages of Structured Social Environments Participants in the current study reported on their experiences within structured social environments, both positive and negative. Positive experiences included an ability to adapt to these environments with ease due to academic success and having set roles and schedules; negative experiences included transitioning to less structured social environments and being inundated with working tasks.

Adapting to structured environments with ease. Nearly half (45%) of the participants expressed adapting to their social environments (i.e., work and school) by demonstrating academic success and adhering to the environment's established structure. Chelsea, when reflecting on her grade school experience, shared: "I was quiet. I sat in the corner. I did as I was told." Andrea elaborated on this sentiment: "I was…gifted…but yeah, like, little did they know that, like, I used that as a coping strategy for how, like, little I actually was able to connect with kids in school." Participants expressed that they excelled in work environments by following directives exactly as they were delivered. For instance, Marica expressed moving up to managerial positions in her previous places of employment because "[when] I was told to do something, I would do exactly how it was told. I was told to do it, and I would get praised for it because it was done perfectly."

Participants who were employed in highly structured, low social environments (18%) reported excelling in their places of employment. Jennifer, who worked as an HR director for a company working with high-profile individuals, shared that "I excel at work…clients like me, and my boss sees that…I'm in an office, and I'm not around others." Similarly, Andrea shared that she was employed as a remote tutor for a child during the pandemic and thoroughly enjoyed it because "I, like, have…a set role." Those who had been in managerial positions (18%), regardless of level of social interaction, also benefitted from constructing their own rules: People had to listen to me when I told them to do something. So, it was kind of like perfect for me, like…I was glad to go to work. It was not really a chore to work.

Everything was how I wanted it because I told people to do it (Marcia). On the other hand, participants who experienced sudden changes in their work schedules reported high-stress levels. Rhea, who works as a contracted tutor through an agency, shared: Recently, I had a change in schedule. I was scheduled originally, for an elementary school, and I had been teaching at that school for a while, for a couple of weeks, and we were already getting towards midterms, so they said I was officially going to be their tutor at that site. And then all of a sudden, last minute, I got moved to a different site that ended up being understaffed, and it was just very difficult because now I have to readjust to the kids and what their needs are, and just kind of a whole situation.

Two (18%) participants also reported thriving under the structure of higher education. As Fatima explained,

> It actually helped me a lot to go back to school…I did my masters. Loved it. It gave me purpose again. It gave me focus. It gave me something to do. I have these readings, I have these papers. I have, you know, it's, I had a regiment that I could kind of recreate again.

Transitioning to less structured social environments. Two (18%) participants, however, felt that higher education provided less structure, thus making the experience more difficult than grade school. Andrea shared,

> I would say it's actually, like, way harder, as, like, opposed to high school, because there's like, less structure in terms of, like, when my day starts, when my day ends, and so I basically have to build my routine like, from scratch every single day, which leads to a lot of decision fatigue and

burnout...[my] brain gets tired from, like, consciously having to make choices every single day.

The other participant, John, shared that his experience at a 4-year university has "been pretty tough" due to the overwhelming number of activities and individuals on campus: "Community college was, like, I kind of saw a lot of the same people, and community college, there's, like, a very small campus…but I think [university] is really big, and there's a lot going on."

"Workaholic" culture. Three of the 11 (36%) participants reported inundating themselves with work tasks. They reported overworking themselves in their place of employment, working in fields they were passionate about. Fatima, a history teacher before her current place of employment, explained:

> I loved the work. I loved being in front of my students because I'm talking about things
>
> I'm passionate about…It just kept me going. But it ended…up affecting [me]. I would
> work too much. I would work too hard. So, I would get home late, I wouldn't call my family…basically, it would become my entire personality.

Similarly, Chelsea, an avid animal lover, expressed having to leave her place of employment after 10 years because, "I couldn't separate myself from the care aspect of taking care of animals."

"We're People Just Like Everybody Else": A Need for More Understanding

Like existing Book, the current study found that feeling misunderstood is a distressing but common sentiment among autistic adults (Crane et al., 2019; Han et al., 2023).

Bullying and isolation. All participants in this study reported some level of difficulty socially connecting with others. Over a third (36%) of participants reported explicit bullying for various reasons such as being overstimulated easily, lack of personal hygiene, and socially inappropriate behaviors. Three (27%) participants reported feelings of alienation, both during and after grade school. Jennifer shared that within her social circle in high school, "it felt more like they were tolerating me than they were my friends. So, I always struggled in school, which is why I dropped out." Rhea–who reported experiencing explicit bullying– also left grade school prematurely due to adverse experiences with other children, opting instead for a virtual schooling program in 11th grade. Fatima, meanwhile, expressed similar sentiments which followed her into graduate school: "even in my master's program, it [was] still clique-y." Furthermore, nearly half (45%) of the sample reported engaging in self-imposed isolation at some point in their lives due to feeling othered.

Autism is a spectrum. Three of the 11 (27%) participants emphasized that ASD is not a monolith. One participant, Andrea, acknowledged the expansiveness of ASD:

> I've…read a bunch of experiences with other people who do have ASD but also, have like, school struggles, etc., etc., because they have like, learning disabilities…but I've also met, like, ASD people who, like, you know, are in college and, like, work a job as well, and, like, are doing pretty okay in school.

The other two participants shared similar sentiments, stating, "You can't really stereotype people" (John) and "autism looks different and feels different and seems different for every person" (Fatima).

Understanding from the general public. Over half (55%) of the participants in this sample emphasized a need for more understanding of ASD from the public. Participants expressed a desire for more understanding surrounding social and communicative difficulties in particular: "We're all like human beings, you know, [we] just like different ways of different like difficulties and like communicating" (John). Rhea elaborated, "We're people just like everybody else…I just kind of wish that at this point in time, people would just view me as just another person, just with you know, that's a little bit different." Participants also expressed a desire for more societal understanding about ASD to educate those who may be undiagnosed themselves: I feel like it needs to be understood more, and I know that sounds like pretty cliche, but it does, because I didn't understand it when I was younger. And if I would have understood what I was going through, I feel like would have been a whole lot easier (Marcia, a 30year-old woman self-diagnosed with ASD at age 27).

Finally, participants expressed a desire for employers to be more understanding of

> ASD: People should know that autism is not a barrier that people can get through it, and if the people can understand, if people that don't understand it get the time and education on how to communicate with those on the spectrum, then I think it'll make people more susceptible to having to working with people with on the spectrum, yeah, and realizing, Oh, they need to take breaks if they're if they're working with an employee [with ASD]

(Chase).

"Social Pressure": Facilitating Socially Appropriate Behaviors

The current study found that autistic adults adhere to socially appropriate behaviors by camouflaging their autistic symptoms and co-regulating, primarily through the help of romantic partners.

Camouflaging. Seven of the 11 (64%) participants reported engaging in camouflaging behaviors. Participants reported that engaging in said behaviors assisted in socially appropriate communication and behaviors. One participant, Jennifer, cited the use of headphones in facilitating her camouflaging:

> [Me and my therapist] were working on, like, me putting on headphones when I go into a store and listen to music, you know, doing things so that I don't feel like I'm in those situations where I'm oversharing.

Another participant, Andrea, reported overcoming her sensory aversion to showering through "social pressure to, like, you know, keep good hygiene…it was out of fear. I was like, [I need to] shower every day." Other methods of camouflaging that participants cited include intentionally keeping conversations balanced and suppressing anger resulting from disruption of repetitive and restricted behaviors.

Co-regulating. Four of the 11 (36%) participants reported co-regulating their autistic symptoms with their identified romantic partners. Two of these 4 (50%) participants noted that their partners were also neurodivergent. One participant expressed gratitude for her partner who assists her in disengaging from unhealthy, restricted behaviors:

> I'm lucky because I have a partner who will remind me to eat and tell me that, you know, it's not healthy to sit for four hours straight…and not let myself go to the bathroom because I don't deserve it yet until I… get through this task (Fatima).

In a similar vein, Paula expressed that her partner encourages her to complete activities of daily living despite her sensory aversions to them:

> I don't like to get into the shower, and then once I'm into the shower, I hate getting out. So there'll be like, days where I'm like, I'm gonna skip the shower today. And you know, like, a couple days will pass my girlfriends, like, you need to shower. Like, that's part of your like, this needs to be part of your daily routine. And, you know, like, I don't know. It just helps for her to list out loud what I need to do.

Isolating. Two (18%) participants also reported isolation to manage their autistic symptoms. John expressed that camouflaging is tiring; to cope, he says, "I try to recharge, just kind of, like, chilling…I kind of find a quiet [place] and like…isolate." Fatima, meanwhile, reported needing to isolate when overwhelmed at her place of employment.

Coping Skills for Autistic Adults With Trauma and Mental Health Concerns

Nine of the 11 (82%) participants in this sample reported external life events that significantly impacted their mental health. Eight of the 11 (73%) participants in this sample reported mental health crises; 4 of the 11 (36%) reported a history of suicide attempts. One participant who reported a history of suicide attempts, Andrea, did not experience any external life events significantly impacting their mental health; instead, she expressed that her three suicide attempts stemmed from "the social deficits, like, part of my life. That was triggering it for me."

Repressing and minimizing major life events. Five of the 9 (55%) participants who had experienced major life events that significantly impacted their mental health reported minimizing or not acknowledging these life events. One participant, Rhea, stated: "I didn't [cope with my trauma]. It was really difficult. I just kind of let it overwhelm me." Similar sentiments were expressed across all five participants, regardless of the nature of the life events that impacted them. These events included childhood sexual abuse, sexual assault, emotional and verbal abuse, parental drug addiction, the death of a parent, child abandonment, and witnessing physical and interpersonal violence.

Independence. Three of the 9 (33%) participants who had experienced major life events that significantly impacted their mental health reported a preference for being or doing things alone. Jennifer, who was in a near-fatal car accident, reported not letting anyone drive her following her car accident. The other two participants reported engaging in self-isolating behaviors, such as going for a drive and taking time off work.

Other coping skills. Other forms of coping with significant life events that significantly impacted participants' mental health included engaging in therapeutic coping skills, special interests, and substance use. Marica, who spoke highly of her mental health care experiences, said:

> The coping skills that my therapist helped me, like stopping and taking a look at what's going on and, before, I like to assess the situation. She just

> helped me, like, really think in the moment to help relieve my anxiety and all that stuff, so I still use all her coping mechanisms now.

Meanwhile, Derek, who shared that he was "obsessed with reading," stated that he "turned to books" when dealing with the fallout of an abusive relationship. Jessie, meanwhile, said: "[I've been doing] coke, things I shouldn't be doing, that's the drinking, smoking, that stuff, [to cope with my trauma]."

Prevalence of Dual Diagnoses

Seven out of the 11 (64%) participants reported a comorbid diagnosis of ADHD. Two of the 11 (18%) participants reported being diagnosed with generalized anxiety disorder, major depressive disorder, PTSD, and bipolar disorder. The findings of this study inform the discussion in Chapter 5.

CHAPTER 5

DISCUSSION

This study sought to explore the relationship between autism in adults, mental health outcomes, and mental health care experiences, focusing on a range of protective factors which protected against severe mental illness. Eleven autistic adults participated in a brief survey measuring current rates of depression and anxiety as well as a 45-60-minute semi-structured interview. Data from the surveys were quantitatively analyzed using SPSS software. Transcripts from the interviews were created and analyzed using Otter.ai software.

Summary of Key Findings

Preliminary research questions were investigated using quantitative data analysis and deductive thematic analysis. No significant relationship was found between age at time of ASD diagnoses and severity of presenting mental health concerns. Furthermore, there was no significant difference in age at ASD diagnosis among gender and race/ethnic identities. However, there was a significant relationship between identified support systems and the severity of presenting mental health concerns: individuals who identified a support system reported higher rates of anxiety at the time of participation. I hypothesize that the correlation exists because of participants' identified support systems not fully understanding their ASD diagnosis. This is corroborated by most participants emphasizing a need for more understanding by the greater public.

Analysis of the interview data found that protective factors against severe mental illness among autistic adults include history of supportive community, current mental health care, and personal resilience. While most autistic adults in the sample reported positive mental health care experiences, reported barriers to accessing mental health care included difficulty obtaining ASD diagnosis, premature termination of services, lack of knowledge about ASD from mental health care practitioners, and internalized stigma. Inductive thematic analysis found that autistic adult participants struggled with emotional regulation, benefitted from structured social environments, desired more understanding of ASD from the public, adapted to socially appropriate behaviors via internal and external factors, possessed varied coping skills, and had a high prevalence of comorbid diagnoses. The current study is unique because it emphasizes how external factors primarily contribute to the mental health outcomes of autistic adults.

The current study found that most participants (73%) experienced mental health crises at some point in their lives. This finding is corroborated by existing Book, which found that 90.7% of autistic adults surveyed had previously experienced mental health problems (Crane et al., 2019). More specifically, all participants who reported a history of suicide attempts (36% of the sample) also reported impaired emotional regulation. This is in line with Richey et al.'s (2015) study, which found that autistic adults with impaired emotional regulation had difficulty modulating emotional responses, thereby increasing impulsivity. This is also akin to Nyrenius et al.'s (2023) findings, which report that 1 in 4 autistic adults have experienced at least one suicide attempt. Moreover, nearly three fourths (73%) of participants in the current study reported comorbid mental health conditions. This is comparable to an existing study where 71% of surveyed autistic adults experienced at least one other comorbid mental health condition (Roestorf et

al.,

2022). The most reported comorbid mental health condition among the current sample was ADHD, with seven (64%) participants disclosing their diagnosis. Similarly, Gilmore et al. (2022) found that 25-38% of autistic adults surveyed had a dual diagnosis of ADHD.

Autistic adults are also more likely to have higher rates of trauma exposure (Hume & Burgess, 2021), which was corroborated by the current study: all but two (82%) participants in the sample reported at least one instance of significant trauma in their lifetimes. Pre-existing research has found social exclusion as a central form of childhood trauma (Brown et al., 2024; Kerns et al., 2022), which was also noted in the current study by a participant.

Eighty-two percent of participants in the current study reported previously seeking mental health care. This statistic bares similarity to Crane et al.'s (2019) study, which found that 90.1% of autistic adult survey respondents had previously sought out mental health care. Existing mental health interventions used with non-autistic patients have been proven effective for autistic adults throughout existing Book (Moore et al., 2024); similarly, participants in the current study who reported benefitting from mental health care reported engaging in traditional mental health interventions during therapeutic sessions. Participants who reported benefitting from mental health care also emphasized the importance of having established rapport with their respective clinicians. They also emphasized the importance of their clinicians' basic understanding of ASD, like findings by Gilmore et al. (2022) and Camm-Crosbie et al. (2019). The protective factors against severe mental illness identified in the current study were also very similar to protective factors identified in the existing Book about autistic adults.

A desire for understanding is the most prevalent theme that arose during inductive thematic analysis, much like Han et al.'s (2023) findings. Participants expressed a desire for understanding within their interpersonal circle and from the public. Several participants hypothesized that feeling understood would lessen their current mental health symptoms. Moreover, some participants expressed that contextualizing their social experiences within the framework of ASD facilitated allowing oneself grace. Participants elaborated that, had they possessed an understanding of their own ASD during childhood and adolescence, they would have more positive mental health outcomes. This sentiment draws parallels to Crane et al.'s (2019) findings, who concluded that the stressors of navigating neurotypical society as an autistic adult led to comorbid mental health conditions.

Limitations

The current study is not generalizable on a grander scale due to its small sample size and lack of control group. Moreover, because of the nature of the research, the interpretation of data is influenced by the research's connection to the information, her existing knowledge, experiences, and unconscious biases as a woman clinically diagnosed with autism. Finally, participants were recruited using snowball sampling within the researcher's personal network and via a key informant who was located at an ethnically diverse university. Therefore, the demographics of the current study are not representative of the autistic adult population at large.

Implications for Future Research

The current study found that autistic adults benefitted from traditional mental health care. Similarly, pre-existing Book found that autistic adults benefitted from mental health interventions modified for autistic adults. However, existing Book does not delineate what these modified mental health interventions may look like. Furthermore, participants in both the current study and in existing Book reported feeling that mental health clinicians are not adequately prepared to work with autistic clients. Thus, future research would benefit from exploring what mental health interventions specific to autistic adults may look like for maximum effectiveness.

CRT and Intersectionality

The demographics of this study differed significantly from national averages. Whereas this study was comprised of seven women (64%), two males (18%), and two nonbinary individuals (18%), national statistics show that American men are over 4 times more likely to be diagnosed with ASD than women (CDC, 2024b). Moreover, previous studies have found that Hispanic/Latine children are the least likely to be diagnosed with ASD (Yuan et al., 2021); however, 2 of the 3 participants who were diagnosed before the age of 18 identified as Hispanic or Latine. Additionally, previous research found that most autistic adults were unemployed (Gray et al., 2014); however, in the current study, nearly 3 in 4 (73%) autistic adults were employed at the time of participation. These differences could be attributed to how the sample for the current study was selected (i.e., scouted through an ethnically diverse, 4-year university). However, the demographics of this study bore resemblance to other studies. The rates of non-heterosexuality among participants in this study are like those found in previous research: McQuaid et al. (2023) found that 41.2% of its sample identified as a sexual minority. Similarly, 64% of participants in the current study identified as a sexuality other than heterosexual.

Implications for Social Work Policy, Practice, and Advocacy

This research identified higher education as a support system for some autistic adults. In the first month of his presidency, President Donald Trump has remarked that he plans to dismantle the U.S. Department of Education. This action would result in, among other consequences, the abolition of federal student aid and an increase in the costs of higher education (Walker, 2025). In turn, autistic adults who depend on financial aid would be deprived of a support system. Moreover, middle-class autistic adults would no longer be able to afford tuition. If autistic adults enrolled at a higher education institution are unable to finish their schooling due to increased costs, the sudden change in routine may be distressing and result in increased mental health symptoms. Social workers should therefore advocate to protect the Department of Education by writing to their elected legislators and working with the NASW to achieve advocacy for autistic adults, who already face significant challenges.

This information is imperative for clinicians working with adult populations. With autism diagnoses among children increasing yearly, it is more likely than not that a clinician will eventually work with an adult client either clinically or self-diagnosed with ASD. Like so, it is crucial for clinicians to inform themselves of mental health struggles and risks unique to autistic adults to best inform their practice going forward with these clients. Doing so aligns with the

NASW's (2017) *Code of Ethics* honoring the dignity and worth of the person while simultaneously emphasizing the importance of human relationships–in this case, strengthening the working relationship between the clinician and the client.

Conclusion

Findings of the current study indicated that autistic adults have elevated rates of mental health concerns. Having established support systems was identified as a protective factor against severe mental illness. However, if this established support system or the greater public lacks understanding of the autistic individual's diagnosis, this support can lead to increased rates of anxiety symptoms. Mental health care experiences overall are generally positive for autistic adults, but existing mental health care can be improved by educating clinicians on ASD, especially among the adult population, and modifying existing mental health interventions for the autistic population. Suggestions for future research include exploring effective interventions for this population and ways to establish psychoeducation among clinicians and the greater public on autism as it presents in adults.